Life Ways

Christ-Believer Relationship

Pictures from Scripture of our relationship with God
By Hugh C. Laybourn

Table of Contents
1. God's Family Pg.2
2. Being One with God Pg.7
3. Living through Christ Pg. 10
4. Passionate desire for God Pg. 13
5. Experiencing total surrender Pg. 17
6. Dependence on Christ Pg. 20
7. Letting Christ be Lord Pg. 22

All rights reserved, copy write: Hugh C. Laybourn

Exploring our relationship with God

Family

> Scripture taken from the *HOLY BIBLE, NEW INTERNATIONAL VERSION.* Copyright © 1973, 1978, 1984 International Bible Society noted as (NIV). Used by permission of Zondervan Bible Publishers.
>
> Scripture taken from the *HOLY BIBLE, NEW KING JAMES VERSION.* Copyright © 1972, 1984 Thomas Nelson, Inc. noted as (NKJV). Used by permission of Thomas Nelson Publishers.

The whole idea that men can have a *personal* relationship with God is an amazing and much-disputed idea among the religions of the world. Many religions feel that the *idea* of God precludes anything personal. In most religions, God is kept distant and impersonal, because he is considered too great to have any contact with mere humans. Many religions teach that in order to know God, we must become perfect, or at least a whole lot better than we are, if we are going to have any kind of relationship with God, the Creator.

As a young Christian I was invited to a church in Boise, Idaho to speak to the youth about what was happening in my life. After I had shared a little of my personal encounter with God, the leader of the church interrupted me, saying I was presumptuous for thinking the Creator of heaven and earth would stoop down to talk to a puny human. He rebuked me for being proud to think that God would be personally involved with me. I sat stunned as I realized that this man, responsible for thousands of others' spiritual lives, was trying to lead them *without* personal direction and guidance from God.

The good news is that God does speak to us and wants us to know him! He wants us to be able to draw near to him. The Apostle Paul wrote:

> Therefore, brethren, having boldness to enter the Holiest by the blood of Jesus, by a new and living way which He consecrated for us, through the veil, that is, His flesh, and having a High Priest over the house of God, let us draw near with a true heart in full assurance of faith, having our hearts sprinkled from an evil conscience and our bodies washed with pure water (Hebrews 10:19-22, *NKJV*).

We can come close to him, "through the veil", by the blood of Jesus Christ. Matt. 27:51 reveals that at Jesus' death on the cross, the veil of the temple was torn, "from top to bottom". The *direction* of the tear of the thick horsehair felt temple veil, or curtain, from *top to bottom* is a picture of God reaching down and ripping open a way for us into the Holy of Holies as Jesus' death re-established God's intimate relationship with man. What a loving God!

What does relationship with God mean? Relationship in its broadest definition means relating with someone or something. The whole idea of being connected or related by some kind of a bond is central to this definition. Can men be connected to the God of the universe? Are we related by blood to the Creator? God the Father has provided, through the blood of his own Son, Jesus Christ, the most amazing and wonderful opportunity for the *created* to connect to *The*

Creator in ways we ordinarily would not and could not be connected. Relationship with God cannot be bought, earned, or demanded. It is an undeserved gift, in the Biblical definition. Relationship with God by any means *other* than by faith in Jesus Christ's provision of forgiveness is unacceptable to God. Jesus said, "I am the way, the truth, and the life. No one comes to the Father except through Me (John 14:6, *NKJV*)."

This intimacy with God is available to everyone who will believe in Jesus Christ. But what we do with this gift of relationship is the choice of every individual. We can feed it and it will flourish; we can ignore it and it will fade. We can pursue it and it will develop; or we can flee it and it will diminish. We can nurture it and it will grow; or we can starve it and it will decline. We can respond to it and it will intensify; or we can react against it and it will slip away. What is your desire? What do you want your relationship with God to become?

I remember as a child my dad, a big 6 foot 4 inch hulk of a man, inviting us to grab his huge index finger and climb onto his size #12 feet as he walked around the room. It was a wonderful game, and we couldn't get enough! Here I was with my chubby little baby fingers hanging on to my father, walking where I couldn't walk and doing what I wouldn't normally be able to do, because I was literally riding on the footsteps of my father! I remember the joy I had as we played this game and the security of knowing that, as long as I held on tight, I would not fall. We also have a 'Father' in heaven that similarly delights in us and he also wants us to walk in

His footsteps. He loves more than any earthly father could, because his love is perfect.

    I would like us to examine the *family* aspect of our relationship with God. In the book of Ephesians, Paul the writer, is praying for the church and clearly voices this family orientation. "…The Father of our Lord Jesus Christ, from whom the whole <u>family</u> in heaven and earth is named…" (Eph. 3:15NKJV.) To be a father you must have children, i.e., sons and daughters who are born or adopted into your family. A family is a social unit created by God. Family relationship was designed by God the Father at creation when the human race began. After God made Adam and Eve, God said to them, "Therefore a man shall leave his father and mother and be joined to his wife and they will become one flesh (Genesis 2:24, *NKJV*)." "Then God blessed them, and God said to them, 'Be fruitful and multiply; fill the earth and subdue it; . . . (Genesis 1:28, *NKJV*).'" This was followed by the birth of Adam and Eve's children to fulfill another part of the destiny of God for their lives. In this first reference in the Bible of family relationships we see some very important things. There is a joining and there is a leaving; there are two that become one; and there is a multiplication of this relationship again and again through their children and their children's children down through the generations. Marriage was a pleasurable, intimate, wonder-filled relationship created by God for the benefit and continuing existence of mankind.

    However, today in the world we have being painted many distorted pictures of family. God, the creator of mankind designed the family, providing a blueprint of how a family should relate and function for all generations. His demonstration of family as the Father of all, is the most correct and accurate picture. I am thankful that the Biblical portrait of family is unchanging and secure.

The Apostle Paul makes it clear that we are part of a *named* family: "... the Father of our Lord Jesus Christ, from whom the whole family in heaven and earth is named (Ephesians 3:14-15, *NKJV*)." What is our family name as believers? The name above all names is the *Lord Jesus Christ*. We share this family name with God the Father, and with Jesus our elder brother. Jesus asked the Father:

> Holy Father, keep through Your name those whom You have given Me, that they may be one as We are. While I was with them in the world, I kept them in Your name (John 17:11-12, *NKJV*).

There are some delightful aspects of family that we might consider in our meditation of our relationship with God. The fact that God is our Father is so wonderful and truly amazing! Conversely, Jesus said to the Pharisees, "You are of your father the devil, . . . (John 8:44, *NKJV*)." But Hosea says, "And it shall come to pass in the place where it was said to them, 'You are not My people,' there it shall be said to them, 'You are the sons of the living God (Hosea 1:10, *NKJV*).'" So when we put our faith in Jesus Christ, the Bible teaches that our Father in heaven adopts us into his family as full-fledged children.

Only Jesus Christ can reveal the Father to us. Jesus said:

> "All things have been delivered to Me by My Father, and no one knows the Son except the Father. Nor does anyone know the

Father except the Son, and he to whom the Son wills to reveal Him (Matthew 11:27, *NKJV*)."

In fact, much to the anger of the religious leaders of his day, Jesus spoke and acted as though this personal relationship with God as Father was not only possible but totally necessary. Because Jesus introduced the idea of God as Father in a personal sense, let's go to him to discover what the character of the Father is.

He loves us as a father should love his kids. Psalms 103:13 says, "As a father has compassion on his children, so the LORD has compassion on those who fear him". (NIV).

The Father in heaven can be touched with the feelings of our weaknesses. As a Father, God is strong and gentle, loving and disciplining, taking great joy in us, but sorrowful when we mourn.

God wants us to be in *the bosom of the Father*. I believe this is a picture of the depth of intimacy we can have with him. In his gospel, John wrote of Jesus, "No one has seen God at any time. The only begotten Son, who is in the bosom of the Father, He has declared Him (John 1:18, *NKJV*)." Jesus was in the bosom of the Father. Philip asked Jesus to show them the Father, and Jesus said to Philip:

> "Have I been with you so long, and yet you have not known Me, Philip? He who has seen Me has seen the Father; so how can you say, 'Show us the Father'? Do you not believe that I am in the Father, and the Father in Me? The words that I speak to you I do not speak on My own authority; but the Father who dwells in Me does the works. Believe Me that I am in the Father and the Father in Me, or else believe Me for the sake of the works themselves (John 14:9-11, *NKJV*)."

By faith we, in Jesus, can also be in the Father. We can be so close to God that we are leaning on His *bosom*, just like John. Speaking of himself at the Last Supper John wrote, "Now there was leaning on Jesus' bosom one of His disciples, whom Jesus loved (John 13:23, *NKJV*)." When your head is resting on the Father's bosom, you can hear his heart beat. You can feel what he cares about and what he is passionate about. What an amazing picture for us to see the depth of the Father's love for us! He loves us as a father should love his kids.

God wants us to know how deeply he loves us and that he is the source of *all things* for us. John the Baptist speaking to his own disciples of Jesus said, "The Father loves the Son, and has given all things into His hand (John 3:35, *NKJV*)." The Father will set his seal on us, (for security), and protect us. He will feed us and care for us. He will fill us with his life and give us a full, quality life in him. Unlike earthly fathers, our Heavenly Father is *always* with us.

God wants us to know that it's right to worship him as Father. Jesus said to the woman at the well:

> "Woman, believe Me, the hour is coming when you will neither on this mountain, nor in Jerusalem, worship the Father. You worship what you do not know; we know what we worship, for salvation is of the Jews. But the hour is coming, and now is, when the true worshipers will worship the Father in spirit and truth; for the Father is seeking such to worship Him. God is Spirit, and those who worship Him must worship in spirit and truth (John 4:21-24, *NKJV*)."

The Father is looking for worshippers. He is looking for those who want a relationship with him. Our relationship with the Father should be so close that we only do what we see the Father do, and we only say what the Father tells us to say. This was true of Jesus as he said, "Most assuredly, I say to you, the Son can do nothing of Himself, but what He sees the Father do; for whatever He does, the Son also does in like manner (John 5:19, *NKJV*)." Jesus lived to please the Father, and our desire should be to follow Jesus' example. If we are relating to God as our personal Father, we will only want to do his will. He will show us what he is doing, even the great works of God. He will speak to us and tell us what to speak to others. We won't need to fear or wonder what to say. God our Father will teach us how to live and what to do. He lives in us and will never leave us alone. What a wonderful Father we have!

      What is faith in God? It is a simple, unreserved trust in God. Faith requires leaning on and depending on Him. Faith is trusting in His Word which contains His promises to us. Trust is very practical in our relationship with the Father in Heaven. Our every waking moment should be lived out of our trust in the Father heart of God. We depend on Christ's sacrifice that secures our relationship with him. God is our Father by the new birth. We are *adopted* into his family by faith in his sacrifice of Jesus Christ. We even take on His name in this adoptive process. We can trust in Him, our Father and our God to lead, guide, and direct our every moment. We, who are justified, "live by faith."

      One thing that is wonderful about children and parents is the trust relationship they have. Children enjoy a wonderful simplicity of faith and trust in their parents. In the same way, we can relate with simple faith and trust in our Heavenly

Father. We, being hidden in Christ, can call God "Abba", or "Daddy", just as Jesus did. What a privilege we have! I remember throwing my sons up in the air and catching them when they were little. They trusted me. I could have accidentally dropped them, but they never doubted for a moment that I would catch them. They laughed and enjoyed the game. In the same way we must trust that our Father in heaven will always catch us. We will not fall, especially when we are putting our confidence in Him.

That God is our Father is almost too wonderful to imagine and truly amazing!

You can pray this prayer right now: Lord, would you reveal your Fatherhood to us? Would you come and remove any false portraits of father and show us how deep and pure and good your Father-love is? I pray for you to make us totally secure in your love and help us to know we are accepted and loved perfectly in your family, for Jesus sake.

EXPLORING OUR RELATIONSHIP WITH GOD
BEING ONE WITH GOD

Jesus came to reveal the Father. Remember when Philip said to Jesus, "Lord, show us the Father, and it is sufficient for us (John 14:8, *NKJV*)." Jesus said, "Have I been with you so long, and yet you have not known Me, Philip?

He who has seen Me has seen the Father; . . . (John 14:9, *NKJV*)." Jesus' mission was to reveal the Father in his character and his nature, and that is exactly what Jesus did.

To the hearts of the hungry this was exciting, but to the hearts of the religious this idea produced anger and even hatred. "Therefore the Jews sought all the more to kill Him, because He not only broke the Sabbath, but also said that God was His Father, making Himself equal with God (John 5:18, *NKJV*.)" Jesus' claim to be God's Son stirred up extreme anger and hatred in the Jewish leaders.

We can see the human analogy of being one with God in the picture of the marriage relationship. In Genesis the physical union between husband and wife is described as the two becoming "one flesh" (Genesis 2:24). In the marriage of two believers, they also become one in spirit. However, notice that there is still something in the two that is *becoming* one. Both their flesh and their souls are *becoming* one. That's why they don't think alike, they don't desire the same things. They're still *becoming* one!

Do any of you have conflicts in relationships? Are any of you married and you see things differently or disagree with your spouse? Any of you? It's because you're still becoming one!

In the same way, if we are believers, we are one Spirit with Jesus in God. We have the same Spirit that raised Christ from the dead in us, and in Ephesians 5:30 the apostle Paul wrote, "For we are members of His body, of His flesh and His bones." We've become married to him, in a sense, as members of the Bride of Christ. But guess what? We're still *becoming* one with Jesus. Because even though we are believers, we've got a lo-o-o-ng way to go to become like Jesus.

John 17 is the key passage about being one with the Father. Jesus prayed, "My prayer is not for them alone, I pray also for those who will believe in me through their message, that all of them may be one, Father, just as you are in me and I am in you (John 17:20, *NIV*)."

We may be Christians, but guess what? It's a process! The process begins by talking about oneness with one another. We begin working through relational issues. Jesus said, ". . . that all of them may be one, Father just as you are in me and I am in you (John 17:21a, *NIV*)." Although it's apparent that we need to be one with each other, we need to one with God first. That process is also happening. Furthermore, we need to be one with one another, *in the same way* as the Father and Jesus were one. Why? Jesus said, "May they also be one in us, *that* the world may believe that you have sent me (John 17:21b, *NKJV*)." This is not some side issue is it? This is an important concept. To be one with God and one with one another is vital!

We are not going to win the world, we are not going to impact the world, unless unity with God and unity with one another exists. In spite of our differences, if we can't learn to love one another, and love authentically, we are not going to change the world. Do you see how important this is in the heart of God? Unless we find out how to walk in unity and walk in love, the world will not believe! The heart of God is throbbing with this message: Jesus came to earth to win the world; Jesus came to turn the world back to Him. Jesus died on the cross to make a way where there was no way.

Jesus' prayer continued, "I have given them the glory you have given me, that they may be one as we are one: I in them and you in me (John 17:22-23a, *NIV*)." How do we become one? It's through the glory! What's going to cause us to come together? What's going to cause us to tear down the walls? What's going to cause us to resolve conflicts? What's going to cause us to forgive one another? What's going to cause us to have this unity? It's the glory of God!

What is the glory? It's Jesus. He is the glory! It's his presence. Becoming one with Jesus is the only way we can ever hope to become one with one another. The more we get filled with the Holy Spirit, the more we connect with the body of Christ.

You know what? Humans are not easy to love. I mean just generally, humans. We can look around the world and say, humans are tough to love. There's some bad stuff going on isn't there? Just open your newspaper and read about it, violence, hatred, rape, abuse, murder. But, "For God so loved the world (John 3:16a)," the whole world. Give me that kind of love, Lord.

I confess to you, I am not there yet. But I want to be there. I need more of the glory. I need more of the life of God in me. I know I'm one with God. I know his life is in me, but I want more of the glory! I need an exchange, because I still see a lot of selfish attitudes, a lot of bad attitudes in my life. Jesus said, "I have given them the glory that you [Father] gave me (v. 22)". You can't buy the glory. You can't work out a deal with God. Jesus settles it in this verse, "I've given them the glory." If the Spirit of God is in you, then the glory is in your life. We just need to let the glory be in charge! We just need the glory of God to bring those changes in us and we need to get out of His way and let the glory be revealed. "I have given them the glory you gave me." Was Jesus glorious?

Yes! Read the gospels again. Jesus is beautiful! He is so gracious! He is so kind! He is so loving! People respond or reject God when they are in Jesus' presence. Such a glorious presence is with Jesus, that it changes the atmosphere. He ruined every funeral he went to, because he would raise the dead. Now that's glory! I'm trying to stir you with a greater desire for intimacy with God. We might know intellectually or theologically that we are one with God, but there is a gap between what we know and what we experience.

The glory of God, the fragrance of God, is not exuding or flowing from us like it did from Jesus. Jesus said, "I in them, and you in me (v. 23)." Just close your eyes for a second and say that with me, "I in them and you in me." Jesus is saying, " I'm going to be in them like you're already in me." So guess who else is in us? The Father is living and abiding in us. Jesus describes this indwelling of the Father in this way ". . . I in them and you in me. May they be brought to complete unity to let the world know that you sent me and have loved them even as you have loved me (John 17:23, *NIV*)." It is a process, isn't it? See, God has created us, God has bought us, and transformed us, that we might exhibit the love of the Father to the world. The people in the world are not going to read the Bible without knowing Jesus, having the Holy Spirit to teach them. They might read the Bible intellectually, but they will not understand it. However, they will read you. You are the one who will exhibit God's glory to the world. You're the one, as you love the unlovely that will reveal Jesus. Something has to happen inside of us so we love one another blemishes and all. There's not one perfect person alive on earth, yet God loves us. Heavenly Father, give us this kind of love for one another, love that loves beyond the blemishes.

First we need to be one with God in intimacy. Second we need to be one with him in proximity. In other words, we need to *hang out with him*. Jesus said, ". . . I am with you always, even to the end of the age (Matthew 28:20, *NKJV*)." We need to be one, in his presence. We need to wake up in the morning and get into God. Don't let the morning start without talking to him, and then walk all day with him.

Third we need to be one with God in security. Jesus said, "My Father, who has given them to Me, is greater than all; and no one is able to snatch them out of My Father's hand (John 10:29, *NKJV*)." In conclusion, be with Jesus, be intimate with Him, find yourself in proximity with God, and abide in Him.

Then build your confidence. Paul wrote in Hebrews 13:5, "For He Himself has said, "I will never leave you nor forsake you." Build your confidence, knowing nobody can pluck you from God's hand. Put your confidence in his strength, his ability, not your own resources.

I'm so glad God is the one who pursued us and grabbed us.
Paul wrote: "There is one body and one Spirit – just as you were called to one hope when you were called – one Lord,

one faith, one baptism; one God and Father of all, who is over all and through all and in all (Ephesians 4:4-6, *NIV*)."

That's where we want to live, every day, with that sense of unity. No matter where we are, there is a presence, a glory. God wants us to be conscious of His presence. Someone defined the fear of the Lord in this way: to have a constant awareness of God's power and presence. I like that. We are one with Him. Let us be continually aware of His presence with us.

Prayer: Father, tear down any barriers between us and you. Thank you for your forgiveness. We want to be one with you and live and dwell in you as you dwell in us, for Jesus sake.

Exploring our relationship with God:
Living in and through in Christ

What a joy it was to purchase our first house! It was a big rambling two-story, turn of the 20th century home. We had been blessed by a retired couple who believed in our ministry and helped us purchase this old apartment house in Walla Walla, Washington. It was a place of ministry and a home, and best of all, it was ours! Our first child, Michael was raised there until he was three or four years old, and then we moved.

God wants us to continually live and dwell in Him. He wants to be our "house" or home to live in. Jesus prayed, "Father, I want those you have given me to be with me where I am . . . and that I myself may be in them (John 17:24a, 26b, *NIV*)." Jesus wants so much to be with us and live in continual relationship with us. What does it mean, *to live in Him*?

God made the universe through Jesus and holds all things together "by the word of His power (Hebrews 1:3)." Therefore, in one sense, everyone *lives in Him.* Paul wrote, ". . . for in Him we live and move and have our being . . . (Acts 17:28, *NKJV*)." But this is certainly not being *in Him* in the intimate sense that Jesus speaks of in the book of John. First Jesus says to Philip, ". . . I am in the Father and the Father in me (John 14:10, *NKJV*)." Then He says, "If anyone loves me, he will obey my teaching. My Father will love him, and we will come to him and make our home [residence] with him (John 14:23, *NIV*)." Earlier, Jesus said, "Before long, the world will not see me anymore [when Jesus returned to heaven], but you will see me. On that day [when Jesus was taken up into heaven] you will realize that I am in the Father and you are in me, and I am in you (John 14:19-20, *NIV*)." Further on Jesus told his disciples, "Remain in me and I will remain in you. . . . As the Father has loved me, so have I loved you. Now remain in my love. If you obey my commands, you will remain in my love, just as I have obeyed my Father's commands and remain in his love (John 15:4, 9-10, *NIV*)."

I have such a hunger to have God make his home in me and to commune with me in that secret, hidden, intimate place with God. I want to know him and be known by him. I know this is possible, because of Jesus, but we seem willing to accept a much lower standard of relationship. We don't seem to live in the full realization of God himself dwelling and living in us. He is a giant of a God, yet he lives in us. He is huge! Why are we not in awe? It should take our breath away to know that the Creator of the universe is living and moving in and through us. Thank you Lord!

God placed a barrier, or veil, between the Jews and His presence in the temple of Moses, separating the Holy of Holies from the place where the people came to worship. Jesus made a way through the *veil*. The tearing of the veil in the temple happened when the body of Christ was *torn* on the cross to restore access to God for all believers. God no longer dwells in temple buildings. When Jesus died and rose again, the bodies of believers became the temple of the living God. We must trust in His amazing provision through the sacrifice of Jesus. <u>By faith in the promise of God, Jesus Christ does live in us, but our choices determine whether we continue to live in Him or exclude Him</u>. This is a delicate balance to be found in God. We invite Jesus in and can make him comfortable by our obedience, or we will drive him out by our bad choices.

Living in Christ is primarily an act of faith in the provision of God through Jesus Christ. We are one with Him through forgiveness of our sins by our faith in the blood of Jesus. We can enjoy a continuing relationship with Him as we say *yes* to him in all things. Every *no* pushes the Lord away. As we walk in obedience to His Spirit, we are doing the things that please the Father and we draw close like Jesus did. The problem arises when we sin, stumble, or miss the mark. A barrier comes between us and God when we go our own way. God and sin cannot dwell together. Therefore we must deal with these barriers on a <u>continual</u> basis to keep the way to God clear.

I don't believe that this means we are constantly checking to see if we are keeping the *rules*. No, God demands a more personal accounting. We have the principles of God's Word to guide us, but he truly wants us to have an *ear to hear* what the Spirit says. He wants a single, focused heart that loves and delights in pleasing him *above all else*. "And if anyone sins, we have an Advocate [defender] with the Father, Jesus Christ the righteous (1John 2:1, *NKJV*)."

God wants us to live acknowledging the Father every moment of every day. Thinking of Him, singing to Him, talking to and walking with him should be our delight. We could sum this up by quoting the scripture: "I in them, and You in Me; . . . (John 17:23, *NKJV*)." Jesus also prays, "Father, I desire that they also whom You gave Me may be with me where I am . . . (John 17:24, *NKJV*)."

Picture living in a home. Different from a house, a home is a personal place, a place with history. Letting down your protective guard, in a home you can be who you really are, transparent and honest. A home is a place of love, relationship, openness, refuge, and security.

According to scripture we are God's temple, God's building. We want our lives to be his *home*, the place where he delights to dwell. Someone moving into a house to make their permanent home is a picture of God coming into our life and taking up residence. The Holy Spirit makes a true home in our hearts. We want him to be delighted to dwell in us. Our life is transparent before God, and he fills our home with love. We are never alone. Wherever we are, we are with him. To live with God is a joy, it is the delight of delights.

We live in him and he lives in us. We dwell in Father's house and he dwells in us.

If fact, we are his house, where he is pleased to abide. We have become, by the blood of Jesus, a place where he is pleased to dwell *forever*.   Paul describes it in this way: "In him the whole building joined together rises to a holy temple in the Lord. And in him you too are being built in a dwelling in which God lives by his Spirit (Ephesians 2:21-22, *NIV*)."

Prayer: Lord, let me be a dwelling place that you are pleased to dwell in. Cause me to turn from anything that pushes you away, for I delight in You.

EXPLORING OUR RELATIONSHIP WITH GOD
PASSIONATE DESIRE FOR GOD

Hunger and thirst have driven men and women to do things that they would never ordinarily do. Here in the Northwest United States we are still haunted by the memory of a group called the "Donner Party" that resorted to cannibalism to try to save their lives in a severe winter trek during the early history of this area.

The Jews thought Jesus was talking to them about cannibalism when they asked him for a sign that they might believe in him.

> They said to Jesus, "Our fathers ate the manna in the desert; as it is written, 'He gave them bread from heaven to eat.'" Then Jesus said to them, "Most assuredly, I say to you, Moses did not give you the bread from heaven, but My Father gives you the true bread from heaven. For the bread of God is He who comes

> down from heaven and gives life to the world. . . . Your fathers ate the manna in the wilderness, and are dead. . . . I am the living bread which came down from heaven. If anyone eats of this bread, he will live forever; and the bread that I shall give is My flesh, which I shall give for the life of the world (John 6:31-32, 48, 51; NKJV)."

The Jews were upset and quarreled, because they thought Jesus was talking about cannibalism. They didn't understand that Jesus was talking about the bread and wine in the Lord's Supper that we now celebrate to remember the redemption from sins that was purchased for us by Jesus' body and blood in his death on the cross. Jesus was not put off by their misunderstanding. He continued to speak to them about their need to eat his body and drink his blood:

> "Most assuredly, I say to you, unless you eat the flesh of the Son of Man and drink His blood, you have no life in you. Whoever eats My flesh and drinks My blood has eternal life, and I will raise him up at the last day. For My flesh is food indeed, and My blood is drink indeed. He who eats My flesh and drinks My blood abides in Me, and I in him. As the living Father sent Me, and I live because of the Father, so he who feeds on Me will live because of Me. This is the bread which came down from heaven—not as your fathers ate the manna, and are dead. He who eats this bread will live forever (John 6:53-58, *NKJV*)."

Even Jesus' disciples thought Jesus was referring to cannibalism, and would not understand until they sat at table at the Lord's Supper. They said, "This is a hard saying; who can understand it (John 6:60, *NKJV*)?" Jesus said to them, "Does this offend you? What then if you should see the Son of Man ascend where He was before? It is the Spirit who gives life; the flesh profits nothing. The words that I speak to you are spirit, and they are life. But there are some of you who do not believe (John 6:61-64, *NKJV*)."

What a powerful motivating force hunger is! Physical hunger will drive people out of their normal existence. Spiritual hunger is just as real, and is a powerful motivating force causing people to seek God. In this fourth meditation about our relationship with God I want to talk about our need for God portrayed by the phrase, "to hunger and thirst for righteousness (Matthew 5:6, *NKJV*)." We very much need to continually seek and follow after God. God wants us to seek Him. David wrote in Psalm 27:4, "One thing I have desired of the Lord, that will I seek: that I may dwell in the house of the Lord all the days of my life, to behold the beauty of the Lord, and to inquire in His temple." Seeking God is a lifetime pursuit.

Hunger and thirst are two of the most basic mechanisms in our flesh. God designed hunger and thirst to trigger desire for our most basic needs. If our bodies were unable to indicate our nutritional needs, we might not care for and feed our bodies properly or sufficiently, and we could very well die of starvation or dehydration. The analogy is powerful. We also have a spiritual hunger and thirst mechanism built into our spirits to propel us towards God. Our spiritual health hinges on our ability to hear God's voice in this area. We must learn to recognize the spiritual hunger within warning us of low God levels in our lives, and the need to feed on his Word, speak to him, and drink in his Spirit more frequently.

The human body's hunger for food is something we all experience. We live with physical hunger every day. In the same way, Spiritual hunger is a natural drive deep within our spirit that causes us to pursue God. His Word is our spiritual food. He is our source of life. We must go to him in prayer daily, continually. God fed the children of Israel in the wilderness. They had to gather the 'manna' daily; they could not depend on yesterday's supply of manna\food. They had to gather their necessary food daily just as we must daily go to God, and seek Him for our sustenance. Are you hungry? Are you thirsty? The picture of thirst for God is the same as the picture of hunger.

Think about how you feel when you are satisfied after a good meal. There is contentment and rest as your body digests the meal. Think about drinking deeply of a cool, refreshing, and satisfying glass of water on a hot day. In the same way we can drink deeply of the Holy Spirit. On the last day of the Feast of Tabernacles, "Jesus stood up and cried out, saying, 'If anyone thirsts, let him come to me and drink (John 7:37, *NKJV*).'" Are you thirsty?

We are sheep in Jesus' fold. We need Jesus just like the sheep desperately need the shepherd to lead, feed, guide, and protect them. In John 10:1-16 there is a description of Jesus, the Good Shepherd. There John writes of Jesus, "He calls his own sheep by name and leads them out (v. 3, *NIV*),"and ". . . his sheep follow him because they know his voice (v. 4, *NIV*)." Often Jesus called disciples to himself by merely saying, "Follow me." The psalmist writes, "We are His people and the sheep of His pasture (Psalm 100:3, *NKJV*)."

Like sheep we are to follow the voice of the great Shepherd. The writer of Hebrews wrote of the great Shepherd:

> May the God of peace, who through the blood of the eternal covenant brought back from the dead our Lord Jesus, that great Shepherd of the sheep, equip you with everything good for doing his will, and may he work in us what is pleasing to him, through Jesus Christ, to whom be glory for ever and ever. Amen (Hebrews 13:20-21, *NIV*).

Jesus will lead us and guide us. He will feed and care for us, *if* we will follow after the Lord. John wrote in Revelation 14:4, "They follow the Lamb wherever he goes (*NIV*)." If you listen in your spirit you will hear that still small voice within calling, "Come, come to me." When we are continually seeking Him we will learn to recognize the gentle voice of the great Shepherd. We will grow in confidence in his guidance and direction.

We see this same principle in the disciple\Master relationship. As believers we are called to be disciples of our Lord and master, Jesus Christ. We learn from the master, we serve the master, and we must obey the master. A disciple learns to be like his master by spending his life following and pursuing his master. Our goal is to observe Jesus' actions and attitudes to become more like him. A disciple is compelled to be with the master to learn and do all he can just like the master.

Elisha and Elijah are good examples in scripture of this dogged pursuit by the disciple. Many times the old prophet Elijah encouraged the young man Elisha to leave him and pursue other things. But Elisha, the young prophet wanna-be, was determined to be with his master Elijah until the end, and

Elisha received the double portion anointing that he requested. We must pursue Jesus Christ with this same determination and passion. Then we, just like Elisha, will receive the promised blessing Jesus has purposed for our lives and callings.

Here are some excellent verses on seeking the Lord. Paul wrote, "Set your mind on things above, not on earthly things (Colossians 3:2, *NIV*)." Pursue God! What we think about the most is what we seek or pursue the most. We are setting our minds on things above when we have our minds filled with the truth, the principles and testimonies in the scripture about God. You are the one who does the setting of your mind. God doesn't set your mind; Satan doesn't set your mind; the world doesn't set your mind. You are not manipulated or victimized when it comes to deciding what you think. You get to choose what you are going to set our mind on. You are the one who controls what you think. If you want to be free from the ways of the world, the lies and deception of Satan, and the lusts of your own flesh, you can choose to think about eternal and spiritual things. Fill your mind with the truth that is in God's Word.

God is looking for men who will seek him. Those who are seeking the Lord will praise him. Praise is one of the most powerful ways we can seek God. As we worship and praise him, we come into that holy place with him. There we can gaze at him and commune with him. We are to seek God for his presence, and his glory. One place to seek him is in his temple. In the spiritual sense, our bodies are his temple. We can seek him in our thoughts, in our heart, in our spirit, and we can serve him with our physical body. We can also join other believers in a building or dedicated place where they gather to seek God. David wrote:

> Taste and see that the Lord is good; blessed is the man who takes refuge in him. Fear the Lord, you his saints, for those who fear him lack nothing. The lions may grow weak and hungry, but those who seek the Lord lack no good thing (Psalm 34:8-10, *NIV*).

If we seek the Lord he promises us that we will lack no good thing. May we all have the same heart as David who sang, "O God, you are my God, early will I seek you; my soul thirsts for you, my flesh hungers for you, as in a dry and weary land where there is no water (Psalm 63:1, *NKJV*)." In truth we are to seek God continually. Are you seeking God with all your heart? Are you pursuing Him? Do you long for Him? Do you hunger and thirst and desire Him? Seek Him and you will find Him!

I have found that there is a great battle to keep us distracted from our relationship with God. Psalm 16:8 has become my theme song: "I have set the Lord always before me. Because he is at my right hand, I will not be shaken (*NIV*)." Knowing that the enemy is working to distract us, we must *make a conscious choice* to set the Lord **always** before us. Three things that accomplish this for me are: prayer, meditation on God's Word and worship/praise. These are powerful tools to dynamite the distractions around us and are great instruments to usher us into his presence. I challenge you to also make these a part of your life and to keep your focus on the Lord.

Prayer: Lord, give me a hunger, a deep craving for you and your presence in my life. Don't let me be satisfied with status quo or just knowing about you. Let m e come to you, face to face. In Jesus name.

Exploring our relationship with God
Total Surrender
King/Servant relationship - Who is your Master?

There are many times in Christian service where someone is required to do something that they don't want to do, but the task must be done. I had an example of this, when, as the overseer of a local church in another town, the temporary pastor tried to take over the church and get control of the property that the churched owned. I was able through very difficult circumstances to stop his attempt and preserve the church and the leaders serving the church. But it was very difficult.

My nature is to not confront, but that day I knew that I had to surrender my will to God and do what he wanted. I had to confront this man and stop the coup. God used the whole experience for good.

In Romans 6: 16-17 Paul writes about being slaves either, ". . . of sin to death, or of obedience to righteousness (*NKJV*)." Each of us has to choose to yield ourselves to God in every circumstance or decision. We let either sin or God, control us. As we present ourselves to God, God can use us as a righteous instrument in his hand. It is a choice and an action on our part: "that to whom we present ourselves slaves to obey—whether sin . . . or obedience . . . (v. 16)." We become just that—*slaves* of one or the other.

It is difficult for those of us in countries where the form of government is democracy, to understand the relationship of a Monarch and the peasants, or slaves. This is a very strong picture. A monarch, or king, has absolute authority over his subjects. His word is law. Whatever the king wants; he gets. What he likes is blessed, and what he dislikes is cursed. Thank God for our benevolent King Jesus!

Slavery, or being a bondservant, requires absolute obedience. A slave must obey their masters or they are punished, often severely. In these cultures disobedience can cost a slave his life. A slave/servant does whatever his master commands. Like the centurion said to Jesus, "I tell this one, 'Go' and he goes; and that one, 'Come,' and he comes. I say to my servant, 'Do this,' and he does it (Luke 7:8)."

Even Jesus had this mindset. In Phil. 2:5-8 Paul wrote of Jesus' humble attitude. Even if it was going to cost him his life, he was willing to please the Father first. He was a willing slave to the Father. Even though he was God's son, Jesus made no reputation for himself, but took on the form of a servant, and became limited as a man. What a sacrifice He made! The Creator of the universe was limited to one puny human body. What humiliation! But it was all to honor the Father. Now, Jesus has his church in which he dwells and walks throughout the earth in a multi-membered body.

In practical terms, serving Jesus as our Master means surrendering every thought, word, and deed to our King, Jesus. It means his wish becomes our command. It means doing what pleases him, no matter how difficult it is or how much it goes against our grain or our desire. It means delighting in the will of God first.

Surrender implies acquiescing to another's control – in this case to the Lord himself. Will we submit our will to his? Will we say like Jesus prayed to his Father in Gethsemane, "not my will, but yours be done (Luke 22:42, *NIV*)." The conflict always comes between our will or desires versus God's will and desire. Whenever this is tested, we must yield.

It is vital for every believer to surrender his will to Christ. We must be like clay in a potter's hands, yielding willingly to being molded, shaped, and transformed by this master potter. It helps to picture God our Father as a gentle but firm potter taking the water of the word, moistening the clay (us) in his powerful, loving hands and shaping us. He works us carefully on the block, cutting us graciously to expose hard places in our lives and to reveal the stones of sin within us. These he removes by casting them away from himself as worthless, when we repent of them. He kneads the clay to bring a consistency in its character. It is then ready for the potter's wheel. To keep the vessel whole and balanced in the thickness of its walls, he must center it and keep it centered throughout the molding process. His design is for every vessel to be reflecting beauty and light. This is only possible as we allow God to take us through the firing process, and then the glazing process. Each experience with fire is necessary for the usefulness and beauty of the vessel. All that is required for this to happen is the total surrender of the clay. He will do the rest.

There are many examples of this principle besides the picture of a potter and clay. The picture of a king and his servant reveals how we are to honor the Lord, allowing him to reign over us by submitting to his place of authority. He is the King, and we are his servants. We must be servants of the King in order to be in his kingdom. We must submit to and obey the sovereignty of God in the earth.

The question of who we obey when we are tempted is clarified by Paul in:

> In the same way, count yourselves dead to sin but alive to God in Christ Jesus. Therefore do not let sin reign in your mortal body so that you obey its evil desires. Do not offer the parts of your body to sin, as instruments of wickedness, but rather offer yourselves to God, as those who have been brought from death to life; and offer the parts of your body to him as instruments of righteousness. For sin shall not be your master, because you are not under law, but under grace (Romans 6:11-14, *NIV*).

We must not let sin be in charge of us, if God is our King. Whoever we submit to, that is our king. What a wonderful motivation to total surrender to the rule of the King of kings.

A beautiful picture of this attitude of surrender is demonstrated when Ruth sneaks into Boaz's tent and lays down at his feet. In mercy and grace he extends his favor to her and then marries her. All the inheritance then goes to and through her lineage all the way to Christ Jesus. This shows the powerful fruit of complete surrender to Him. He will take us as aliens, like Ruth, and will wed us to himself and bless us with every spiritual blessing, in Christ Jesus.

If we don't obey Jesus, we are our own kings. We are subjects of Jesus' kingdom, if we believe and obey him. Jesus said, ". . . the kingdom is within you (Luke 17:21, *NIV*)" and "I confer on you a kingdom, just as my father conferred one on me (Luke 22:29, *NIV*)."

The kingdom of God therefore is a spiritual realm. We enter it by faith in the blood of Jesus Christ and accepting the provisions of the New Covenant. We remain in his kingdom by saying, "yes," to God in thought, word and deed.

Through the revelation of the omnipresence of God and through Christ's power we are able to dwell continually in God's kingdom come to earth. God's kingdom is men and women allowing God to rule, guide and direct them day by day on this planet while willingly submitting to God's will and purpose for their lives.

Have you surrendered to your King and Master Jesus? Have you determined in your heart to live for him and to obey his every wish? See the King, high and lifted up and bow your knee in allegiance to the Lord of lords and the King of kings. Live to please him and you will live life to the fullest!

Prayer: Lord, I surrender my will to you. Lead me and guide me, and use me as you see fit. I surrender to you for the glory of Jesus and for the expansion of your kingdom. Amen.

Relationship with God:
Dependence on Christ

Picture a glove lying on the table. It sits there without moving, no matter what the need, no matter what we say to it. It can't do anything until it is placed on a hand. In the same way it is absolutely impossible for us to do anything without Christ Jesus living in and through us. We can't love without him, we can't overcome without him, nor can we succeed without him. We need his power and life to come into our lives so we can accomplish what he wants us to accomplish.

When we allow him to fill us there is life and power within us like a hand in a glove. Whatever the hand can do the glove can do. Wherever the hand goes the glove goes. It is impossible to live the Christian life without the power of the life of God living in us and working through us. I am amazed at how many people try to live like Christ as if he was only a pattern of the best of humanity, rather than the miracle working Son of God who purchased life for us and gave us his life so we could truly live. As a picture and in practicality this is very clear in scripture.

Jesus said, "I am the vine, you are the branches. He who abides in Me, and I in him, bears much fruit; for without Me you can do nothing (John 15:5, *NKJV*)." The life of the branches comes through the vine or main stalk of the plant. Our life also comes through Jesus our vine. We know that the nutrients of most plants come first through the roots and then through the vine/stalk to the extremities of the plant. We are the extremities. The roots draw from the earth all the nutrients and water necessary for life. Jesus explained what happens if we do *not* abide in him, "If anyone does not abide in Me, he is cast out as a branch and is withered; and they gather them and throw them into the fire, and they are burned

(John 15:6, *NKJV*)." If a branch gets cut off from the main vine it will soon die. There is absolutely no way for a branch to survive on it's own without a continual vital connection to the vine and the roots. Our every thought and deed must proceed from Him. When Satan tempted Jesus, Jesus answered, "Man does not live by bread alone, but by every word that proceeds from the mouth of God (Matthew 4:4, *NKJV*)." God's words bring life to us through him. We do not in ourselves have the power to live the way we should. We need God's help to live in obedience to his commandments. Paul wrote, "For what the law was powerless to do in that it was weakened by the sinful nature, God did by sending his own Son in the likeness of sinful man to be a sin offering (Romans 8:3, *NIV*)." We are also unable to exhibit the character of Christ without God's Spirit working deeply in us. To live a holy life we must live by the power of the *Holy* Spirit in utter reliance on him. In John 15 there are several aspects of the *plant* imagery of relationship with the Lord. In verse two we see the need for pruning the plant, "He cuts off every branch in me that bears no fruit, while every branch that does bear fruit he trims clean so that it will be even more fruitful." In verse four, we see the need for abiding or staying in him, "Remain in me, and I will remain in you. No branch can bear fruit by itself; it must remain in the vine." Then also in verse four and five we see our utter dependence on Christ for all things, for both life and any fruitfulness. Finally, Jesus says, "This is to my Father's glory, . . . (v.8)!"

    There are two aspects of this walk. Because we still have the freedom of choice, we must resist the desires of the lower nature, the flesh, and at the same time yield to or draw on the power and life of the Holy Spirit that lives in us. As Paul writes, ". . . clothe yourselves with the Lord Jesus Christ, and do not think about how to gratify the desires of the sinful nature (Romans 13:14, *NIV*)." In his letter to the Colossians Paul wrote, "If then you were raised with Christ, seek those things which are above, where Christ is, sitting at the right hand of God. Set your mind [*affections* in *KJV*]on things above, not on things on the earth (Colossians 3:1-2, *NKJV*)." We must be actively resisting *and* actively pursuing in order to live in and through Christ.

The prophet Isaiah compared us to oaks, "They will be called oaks of righteousness, a planting of the Lord for the display of his splendor (Isaiah 61:3, *NIV*)." We are like trees planted and rooted in Jesus. This is a great picture of our relationship with God. We are the "planting of the Lord". Referring to Gentile (non-Jewish) believers, Paul wrote, ". . . and you, being a wild olive tree, were grafted in among them (Jewish believers), and with them became a partaker of the root and fatness of the olive tree (Romans 11:17, *NKJV*)." We have been grafted into Christ. Our roots must go down deep into God. He is our nutrient. We must draw all our spiritual nutrients from him alone and drink deep of the "living water" that Jesus offers through the Holy Spirit: "'If anyone thirsts, let him come to Me and drink. He who believes in Me, as the Scripture has said, out of his heart will flow rivers of living water.' But this He spoke concerning the Spirit, whom those believing in Him would receive, for the Holy Spirit was not yet given, because Jesus was not yet glorified (John 17:37-39, *NKJV*)." All this occurs through the 'roots' we have in Christ: the deeper the roots, the larger the tree and the stronger the tree. Water, right nutrients, and sunlight speak of the baptism of the Holy Spirit, the scriptures, prayer, and worship, respectively. We need to be filled with the Holy Spirit, feed on God's word, drink in his life in prayer and bask in His presence in worship in order to be healthy and grow.

    The ability to live like Christ is dependant on our ability to let his life live in and flow through us. Can we surrender to the life of his Spirit. Will we stay in the *flow* of the river of *living water* of God that is in us. His desire for us is to be "united with Him." Paul wrote, "If we have been united with him in his death, we will certainly also be united with him in his resurrection. For we know that our old self was crucified with him so that the body of sin might be rendered powerless, that we should no longer be slaves to sin– . . . (Romans 6:5-6, *NIV*)." As we are "united with him" daily we can draw on his life and power: this is the grace of God.

Paul wrote to encourage the churches, ". . . continue to live in him, rooted and built up in him, strengthened in the faith as you were taught, and overflowing with thankfulness (Colossians 2:6-7, *NIV*)." Pray this prayer with Paul. He included you when he prayed for all believers throughout the generations:

> For this reason I kneel before the Father, from whom his whole family in heaven and on earth derives its name. I pray that our of his glorious riches he may strengthen you with power through his Spirit in your inner being, so that Christ may dwell in your hearts through faith. And I pray that you, being rooted and established in love, may have power, together with all the saints, to grasp how wide and long and high and deep is the love

of Christ, and to know this love that surpasses knowledge—that you may be filled to the measure of all the fullness of God.

Now to him who is able to do immeasurably more than all we ask or imagine, according to his power that is at work within us, to him be glory in the church and in Christ Jesus throughout all generations, for ever and ever! Amen (Ephesians 3:14-21, *NIV*).

Prayer: Lord, I need you. I am so dependent on you and the life of your Holy Spirit. Would you fill me fresh again today? I'm thirsty!

Exploring our relationship with God:
Lordship of Jesus Christ.

What does Christ being Lord in a believer's life really mean? It does not mean that we become robots without a free will, without freedom to choose, without a mind, or without a personality. We do not lose consciousness while serving the Lord. God does not grab us and force us to do his will. He wants us to willingly surrender to his sovereignty in our lives. He wants us to present ourselves as living sacrifices to God as Paul wrote: "Therefore I urge you, brothers, in view of God's mercy, to offer your bodies as living sacrifices, holy and pleasing to God—which is your spiritual worship. Do not conform any longer to the pattern of this world, but be transformed by the renewing of your mind. Then you will be able to test and approve what God's will is—his good, pleasing and perfect will (Romans 12:1-2, *NIV*)." The Lordship of Christ is also not a dictatorship, where Jesus dictates rules for us to follow. God has given himself to us so that we can walk in newness of life. The Holy Spirit provides the power in us through the gospel to live out the life he requires of us. Paul wrote, "For I am not ashamed of the gospel of Christ, for it is the power of God to salvation for everyone who believes, for the Jew first and also for the Greek. For in it the righteousness of God is revealed from faith to faith; as it is written, *The just shall live by faith* (Romans 1:16-17, *NKJV*)." In Colossians 1:27 Paul wrote, ". . . Christ in you, the hope of glory." We live by faith not by rules. We live by the power of Christ working in us not by external controls. The Lordship of Christ does not mean being led about by every voice and whim that comes to us, but rather with a knowledge and confidence we follow the inner voice of the Holy Spirit. It is true that we must test the spirits, so we won't be deceived. John warned us, "Beloved, do not believe every spirit, but test the spirits, whether they are of God; because many false prophets have gone out into the world (1 John 4:1, *NKJV*)." The best way to test the spirits is to be well founded in God's Word. God's Holy Spirit will always agree with God's Word, and He will not apply it out of context. Finally, it is not a straining and working of the flesh to do God's will in an effort to please Him. Paul wrote, ". . . those who are in the flesh cannot please God (Romans 8:8, *NKJV*)." Paul invited believers to enter into the rest of God, ceasing from our own works:

> There remains therefore a rest for the people of God. For he who has entered His rest has himself also ceased from his works as God did from His. Let us therefore be diligent to enter that rest, lest anyone fall after the same example of disobedience. For the word of God is living and powerful, and sharper than any two-edged sword, piercing even to the division of soul and spirit, and of joints and marrow, and is a discerner of the thoughts and

intents of the heart. And there is no creature hidden from His sight, but all things are naked and open to the eyes of Him to whom we must give account. Seeing then that we have a great High Priest who has passed through the heavens, Jesus the Son of God, let us hold fast our confession. For we do not have a High Priest who cannot sympathize with our weaknesses, but was in all points tempted as we are, yet without sin. Let us therefore come boldly to the throne of grace, that we may obtain mercy and find grace to help in time of need (Hebrews 4:9-16, *NKJV*).

Some definitions would be helpful in understanding what Christ being Lord in us means. If we live in a democracy, we are used to having a say in the formation of laws. The moral strength or weakness in a democracy determines the legal framework for the society in which the majority rules. Unlike a democracy, in a kingdom the head of state, or leader of the government of the country, is the king. Jesus is the ruler of the Kingdom of God, the nation of spiritual Israel. Referring to Jesus, the Messiah, Isaiah wrote, ". . . the government shall be upon His shoulder (Isaiah 9:6, *NKJV*)." We are in the kingdom headed by King Jesus. In John's revelation ". . . there were loud voices in heaven, saying, 'The kingdoms of this world have become the kingdoms of our Lord and of His Christ, and He shall reign forever and ever (Revelation 11:15, *NKJV*)!'" Paul also wrote of the kingship of Jesus and his pre-eminence over all other kingdoms:

> He has delivered us from the power of darkness and translated us into the kingdom of the Son of His love, in whom we have redemption through His blood, the forgiveness of sins. He is the image of the invisible God, the firstborn over all creation. For

> by Him all things were created that are in heaven and that are on earth, visible and invisible, whether thrones or dominions or principalities or powers. All things were created through Him and for Him. And He is before all things, and in Him all things consist. And He is the head of the body, the church, who is the beginning, the firstborn from the dead, that in all things He may have the preeminence. (Colossians 1:13-18, *NKJV*).

Sovereign, (derived from the Latin language, meaning above or over), means above, or superior to all others, the greatest. When used in reference to a person, sovereign means someone who is supreme in power, rank or authority; someone who is holding a position of a ruler. <u>Jesus</u> is above all, superior to all others, and the greatest. Jesus Christ is supreme in rank, power and authority. He holds the position of ruler of the universe. He is truly above all!

The word dominion refers to ownership. It means supreme authority or control. The word domain refers to the territory, empire, or land under a government's or ruler's control. We are under the supreme dominion, authority and control of Jesus Christ our Lord and King. We are Jesus' domain by right of ownership. We belong to him, purchased by his blood.

Primarily, therefore, the Lordship of Christ, means Jesus is in control. God wants to sanctify our whole being, body, soul, and spirit. Paul wrote, "Now may the God of peace Himself sanctify you completely; and may your whole spirit, soul, and body be preserved blameless at the coming of our Lord Jesus Christ. He who calls you is faithful, who also will do it (1 Thessalonians 5:23-24, *NKJV*)." Sanctify means to set apart something for holy purposes. God wants to reserve us blameless to the coming of our Lord Jesus Christ. God desires to be in control of our whole being as we present ourselves to Him. As Paul wrote:

> I beseech you therefore, brethren, by the mercies of God, that you present your bodies a living sacrifice, holy, acceptable to God, which is your reasonable service. And do not be conformed to this world, but be transformed by the renewing of your mind, that you may prove what is that good and acceptable and perfect will of God (Romans 12:1-2, *NKJV*).

We must acknowledge that Jesus is Lord and King over all flesh, including ours. Christ has been given authority over our bodies. Speaking of this Jesus said to his Father in prayer, ". . . You have given Him [the Son, or Jesus] authority over all flesh, that He should give eternal life to as many as You have given Him (*NKJV*)." God clearly has given Jesus authority over all mankind. Paul states, "Therefore put to death your members which are on the earth: fornication, uncleanness, passion, evil desire, and covetousness, which is idolatry (Colossians 3:5, *NKJV*)." This challenges us. However, we can only put our flesh to death, because we, in Christ, have been given the authority to do so. According to Paul, we must ". . . put on the Lord Jesus Christ, and make no provision for the flesh, to fulfill its lusts (Romans 13:14, *NKJV*)." Paul declares, ". . . I discipline my body and bring it into subjection, lest, when I have preached to others, I myself should become disqualified (1 Corinthians 9:27, *NKJV*)." How can we make Christ Lord over our bodies, our flesh? We do it by presenting our bodies as living sacrifices to God (Romans 12:1-2), and by embracing the fruit of the Holy Spirit of self-control in our lives (Galatians 5:22-23). Our bodies contain our physical senses with which we sense the world around us.

The enemy would like us to walk and live by the information given to us by our five senses, but this is not faith. Paul clearly stated, "The just shall live by faith (Romans 1:17, NKJV)."

Also, Christ, "the author of our salvation (Hebrews 5:9, NKJV)," "the author and finisher of our faith (Hebrews 12:2, NKJV)", and the one who told Nicodemus, "You must be born again (John 3:7, NKJV)," rules over our spirit. It is through our spirit that is one with his by our faith, that Jesus leads and guides us. It is through his Holy Spirit in us that he empowers us to resist sin. Jesus is Lord in the spiritual realm. There he is clearly King. And all other spirits are subject to Jesus, even the fallen spirits.

Concerning our innermost being, Jesus will rule over our souls as we give him permission. Amazingly he has given us the gift of free will. We can choose to surrender to his Lordship or not. Jesus will not lord it over us (see Matthew 20:28). You or I must choose to make him Lord over our own soul. We must submit to his rule in our lives on a daily basis.

Jesus' Lordship means a daily, moment-by-moment surrender of your self to his leading. This attitude of humility to his control is essential to hearing the subtle promptings of the Holy Spirit.

Once as my wife and I were seeking to find God's will concerning where He wanted us to move, I called a friend about moving to his city. Although he didn't seem to be very encouraging, as I spoke to him I felt a *flutter* of the Holy Spirit's touch upon my spirit, like the touch of a butterfly's wing on my soul. It was so gentle and quiet, yet there was *something*. As we continued to pursue the Lord in this matter, we eventually did move to his city, and we were there in the exact timing of God. God used us to help many people there.

I believe that as long as we are truly willing to do whatever God wants us to do we will be exactly in the will of God for our lives for that time. When we are unwilling to do God's will, we resist him. When we resist him, we delay God's blessing in our own life, and God cannot use us to accomplish what he called us to do. If we resist him long enough, God will call another to do the work in our place.

Every relationship must be tested. Someone may say, and believe, that Jesus is Lord of their life, but God will test their commitment so the person will know what is in their heart. God will put circumstances in their path that will make them choose between doing his will or their own will. It may be something that will cause them to be uncomfortable or embarrassed; it may be something they would never do normally. As we submit to Jesus' Lordship and obey the prompting of the Holy Spirit we will not only accomplish great things, we will please the Father and bring glory to him.

I pray that these pictures of how we relate to Jesus will stir us to draw closer and closer to him. Jesus used such practical examples to demonstrate the kind of relationship he desires us to have with him. Seek the Lord while he may be found.

Ever hungry for Jesus, Hugh.

Made in the USA
San Bernardino, CA
26 January 2018